CW0621426

Text retold by Lois Rock
Illustrations copyright © 1997 Cathy Baxter
This edition copyright © 1997 Lion Publishing

The author asserts the moral right to be
identified as the author of this work

Published by
Lion Publishing plc
Sandy Lane West, Oxford, England
ISBN 0 7459 3832 9

First edition 1997
10 9 8 7 6 5 4 3 2 1 0

A catalogue for this book is available
from the British Library

Library of Congress CIP data applied for

Printed and bound in Singapore

This retelling is based on the stories of Jesus' life in the Bible,
in the Gospels of Matthew, Mark, Luke and John.

The Gentle Carpenter

Retold by Lois Rock
Illustrated by Cathy Baxter

Long ago, in a town called Nazareth, lived a gentle carpenter. His name was Jesus. He worked with wood and stone.

People talked about Jesus.

There were stories about when he had been born.

"Odd stories," they said. "His mother, Mary, says she saw an angel. She says the angel told her she was going to have a baby, who would be God's son.

"She says angels sang on the night he was born."

"She says important people from far away gave the baby gifts—rich gifts for a king."

"But can you believe that God would send his son to work as a carpenter in Nazareth?"

People agreed that Jesus seemed quite nice and normal.

"He grew up a good son, they agreed. "He sticks to his work."

"Once, years ago, he got his mother worried. You remember: a crowd of us went to Jerusalem at festival time. When we started back, Jesus wasn't with us."

"But they found him in the temple in the end. He was talking about God with all kinds of clever people. They said Jesus was a very wise young man."

"Yes. It does seem that God is very important to Jesus."

God was very important to Jesus.

One day, he stopped being a carpenter.

He began to spend his days telling people about God.

He talked to anyone who came to listen: rich and poor, young and old; the kind of people you never saw making a mistake and the kind of people who always seemed to be in trouble.

He listened when people asked questions.

He was kind and gentle with little children.

Jesus told stories.

"Imagine youself in this story," he once said.

"You're a shepherd. You have a hundred sheep and one gets lost.

"What do you do?

"Of course! You go and look for it.

"You look high and low, far and wide... until you find it. Then gently you bring it home.

"God is like that shepherd.

"God looks for those who feel lost...
who always get things wrong...
who long to feel safe and loved."

"Imagine a family," said Jesus. "One day, the youngest child says, 'I'm grown-up now. I'm going to leave home.'

"And he goes and gets into all kinds of good-for-nothing, time-wasting, money-spending trouble.

"When all the money is gone, the child is sorry and thinks: 'What a mistake I made. I'm going home.'

"Every evening, his father has been waiting and watching, waiting and watching. When he sees the child, he runs to welcome him."

People saw that Jesus was telling them about God:

God loves them, whatever they have done. God is like a kind parent: gentle and forgiving and welcoming.

"How can we live as God wants?" people asked.

"Number one," said Jesus, "love God.

"Number two: love other people. Be as good to them as you are to yourself."

"But what if they're horrid to me?" asked one of Jesus' friends. "What if they let me down? What if they hurt me? What if they tease me? What if they cheat? How many times do I forgive them?"

Jesus answered, "You must forgive them over and over and over and over again...

"You must go on loving them
and ask God to do good things for
them.

"Just remember how much God has
forgiven you,
and how much God loves you."

Jesus did more than talk about God and God's love. Jesus did things with God's help to show God's love in action. "He makes lame people walk," people said.

"He makes blind people see."

"He even brings dead people back to life!"

People saw that where there was pain and sadness, Jesus gave people hope and happiness.

It seemed that the whole world was a nicer place when Jesus was there.

One night, Jesus was out in a boat with his friends.

A storm blew up, and they were very afraid.

Jesus spoke to the wind:
"Hush."

Jesus spoke to the waves:
"Be still."

And they obeyed.

"Who is this Jesus?"
his friends asked.
"Who can he be?"

With Jesus, there
was peace and safety.

Jesus had many friends but other people were angry with him. "Who is this Jesus?" they stormed!

"How dare he say the things he says about God? How can he do the things he does?"

"It's not right!"

"We don't like it!"

And they
whispered
and plotted
and planned
and lied
and had Jesus
put to death: nailed
to a cross of wood.

Jesus' friends wept.

They put him in a grave.

It seemed like the end of the story.

But three days later when they went to the grave it was empty.

Once again, people talked about Jesus.

Now there were stories about when he died.

"Odd stories," people said.

"His friends say there was an angel by the grave.

"Or was it two?

"They say they saw Jesus alive.

"They say Jesus gave them a job to do:

to tell people that God loves them,

to tell people that God forgives them,

to tell people that God will give them
new life

and keep them safe for ever."

And people believed them. It made them happy to think God loved them.

They began to love one another.

They really believed that the man who was once the gentle carpenter of Nazareth was God's son come to make them God's friends.